||||| |||| ||| |||| ||| |||| ||||| |||| |||||
I0190507

THE WILD YOUTH.

Poetic adventures in gender identity, mental health, addiction, and being a wild youth.

http://rexemersonjackson.ca

Dedication

For everyone who has ever felt unseen, weird, crazy, or strange.
Be proud. We are family.
      - Rex Emerson Jackson

"We are the reckless, we are the wild youth, chasing visions of our futures. One day we will reveal the truth – that one will die before he gets there."
      -    Youth, by Daughter

TABLE OF CONTENTS

Let Me Out

risk
maybe I am
going to lose
everything.

risk
I can't be this
girl
any more.

risk
I am trapped
inside this
box

and my heart
thunders
within the cage
of my ribs

please
let me out
a plaintive
wail

as everyone smiles
at the little girl
wearing her dress

and pleating her hair

didn't you know
that
little
girl
never existed?

There Is No Boy Here

Spring of Grade 12.
Today was going to be the day
the day I finally nailed it
my biggest role ever:
teenage girl.

Someone smiled at me in the hall
and I wondered
hey, do you see me?

Not the straight little
mousy girl
too afraid to smile back

but the boy?
No. There is no boy here.

All along I longed to
be the chivalrous knight in shining armour.
Hold open the door.
Carry the heavy things.

Not because girls are weak
but because I was enamoured
with these creatures who were
at home in their own bodies
while I wasted a girlhood
angry at the world.

There is no boy here.

Unless.
unless you count the dinosaur I snuck
from my brother's toy box.
I loved lego and matchbox cars
but I played with Barbies.

There is no boy here
unless you count the man who grew up
wearing the clothes of someone else
until one day it was too much
and he shed his female skin
his female name
his female expectations

There is no boy here.
No. But, there is a man.

Pride

it opens like a flower
each petal unfolding
and the new bud
has finally bloomed

I waited through the winter
the cold frozen ground
locking me inside

but it opens like a flower
my heart
my radiant, refulgent heart
winter is over.

I waited through the spring
as all the other shoots bloomed
it wasn't my time yet

and it opens like a flower
my own shape
gender expression be damned
I have come into my own

No longer am I shrinking
No longer am I afraid
of the rhythms
of my body

It opens like a flower
each petal unfolding
and the new bud
is alive.

Judge

my life
my love
my leanings
are not for you to judge

my fate
my fault
my failings
nobody would begrudge

I am not
broken.

I am not
whole.

I am a work in progress.

my self
my song
my secrets
released without a nudge

I am not
broken.

my life
my love

my leanings
are not for you to judge.

What If?

what would even happen
if I were to crawl into bed
somewhere in the heaviness of sleep
would I descent through the mattress
and have midnight parties with
the dust bunnies?

and even if I managed the
elusive dream state
would I traverse my reality
and visit someone new,
maybe someone
who is more me
than I am?

what would happen to my
blanket-wrapped form
warm and inert?
where do the thoughts go
that you don't remember having?

maybe at night we go to this
garden of unremembered ideas
and choose something to
perseverate on
so that when the form in the blankets
opens his eyes
you can see the sheen

of midnight philosopher
leave his body behind as he
bathes in the
red glow of morning

and the heavy, cotton
quiet time
gives way to the
frenetic bustle
of another day.

Dear Body

Dear Body:
I am sorry.
I was supposed to live in you
And instead I drifted somewhere else.

Dear Body:
Can you believe that at one point I thought
I could mold you like Playdoh?
Make everyone gasp in amazement
As you simply
Disappeared?

Dear Body:
I was reckless.
Dear Body:
I was young.

Dear Body:
I never thought anything could hurt you
More than you had already been hurt.
I thought that if I controlled the hurt
I was winning.

Dear Body:
I take the medicine
That protects my mind
And you get polluted in the process.

What's worth more?
Sound mind
Or sound body?
Because some people can't have both.

Dear Body:
I will no longer deny you a voice
You are more than my shell
You are my armor
You are how I feel,
See,
Bleed.

Dear Body:
I am so sorry.

wonderful/terrible

sometimes things are so wonderful
and sometimes things are
wonderful/terrible
horribly beautiful
and it smothers me
because it is
so many things
that I
can't
breathe.

I've never really
subscribed to binaries
male and female
good and evil
horrible and wonderful

there is too much grey
too many feelings
too much potential.

sometimes things are
wonderful/terrible
but I love it
because I am
alive.

strange little girl

spine
tall?
not at all

so many years of
pretending

well, you're a
strange little girl.

so she hunched
into herself
hid that
budding chest

puberty is extra fun
when it feels like your body is
betraying you.

that biological clock will
tick
tick
tick.

ribs
tight?
yes that's right

smothered in a world of
pretty pink
and posters of
cute boys

all he wanted was to embrace
one
pretty
girl

maybe

it's not
too late.

Remnant

I watched the pot boil
tippy toes peering at the stove
6 years old
learning
women's work.

Cross-stitching, sewing
Nana taught me to knit
and I did it because
I loved her so much.

I made a stuffed kitty
in home-ec
I hated that
scruffy, lop-eared reminder
that I was
seen as female.

Expected to do female things.
I wanted to fly a plane.
I wanted to fight fires.

I wanted to be a boy.

Rubber dinosaurs
I delighted in making plastic bugs

I stole my boyhood

in bits and pieces
when no one was watching.

The first time someone saw the real me
was in karate class.
Wearing a sparring helmet,
the instructor took me for a boy
and it was like a firecracker
exploded in my heart.

This is who I am.
And every day,
I fight.
One day,
I'll win.

sometimes the darkness

sometimes the darkness
sits there
mocking me
it doesn't encroach
on my daylight
but instead
broods nearby
just so I
don't forget.

my heart lurches
and stills
the walls thickening
the beats easing
and poetry
poetry
breaks open
this silent world
sends my words
into the quiet
and music
music
quickens the blood
and the iridescent
prismatic
sound
tells the story
of my life.

Spectra

can't you see
the spectra?
so many colours
infinite variabilities

I am not just man
I was not just woman
I am never going to arrive
at a terminus.

I am forever in flux
forever travelling
picking up hitchhikers
along the way

some for a time
some forever
we travel as one
not man
not woman

human.

Abandon

sometimes I feel
my youth so keenly
it slices like a
blade across my throat.

I am one part
foolish
and one part
wise,
perhaps my
childhood has passed.

but I feel the years
I never let myself live
call me back

I'm
not
old
yet.

and as I begin one more
reckless slide
in the early
waking dawn

I hum a melody
that quickens my heart

and twists my guts
with the desire
to be
alive.

never mind the hour
never mind the year

It is not too late
to live with
wild
abandon.

Not While I Can Still

I want to go back
to when I never had these thoughts
but then,
was I ever really innocent?

melancholy
has always been my
closest friend.

these insistent ideas
visceral images
are so much a part of me
but still they are hard
to accept.

so much time spent
waiting for the end to come
so much dread
and so much longing

but I am not its suitor
I do not wish for its hand
we are brief lovers
meeting breathlessly
in the middle of the night
but I don't sleep over

I wonder how it might look

the morning after
would it be triumphant,
having captured me at last?

that is why I never stay in the same place
for too long
I will not give it a chance
to know me

I will not give up.
It will not win.
Not while I can still write
my own story.

Potential

a sharp cry
hits the air
like a wounded animal

or at least,
I think I hear it

perhaps it is only my mind
stretched thin
cerebral cortex
occipital lobes
and cerebellum

flattened under the weight
of everything I have ever been
and everything I have left to do.

must my brain always be either
humming with electric potential
or wrapped in heavy cotton?

such a promising young person
reduced to this?

I have something to say.
So say it.

I am a prodigy

and a failure
all at the same time

Schrödinger's got nothing on me.

driven by circumstance
to set the bar so high
and sometimes when I'm soaring
I clear it with ease
and sometimes my feet
are encased in cement
and I crash face first
knocking out
any
stars
from my
eyes.

All Mad

I live a life of fairytale
bouncing back and forth between
over the rainbow, and
down the rabbit hole

funny,
I've always been drawn to
and horrified by
tornadoes.

a flurry of winds turn my
sepia-toned world into
technicolour
and I marvel at the
vibrancy
every fibre of me alive

until suddenly the storybook changes
and I'm down
thrust into a world
that I am both too large
and too small for.

late
for a very important date.

nothing fits,
everything is just a little

unreal.

And then sometimes it is both at once
a vibrant, technicolour world
that I am too big to fit into
and my voice comes out
both flat and tangential

but don't worry.
We're all mad here.

Dancing Star

there's a supernova in my chest
and I can't stop the words
flowing up my throat
and through these lips
the glorious, generous
verse and phrase
bursting from me

Nietzsche said:
one must still have chaos in oneself
to give birth to a dancing star

my star turns pirouettes
it leaps like a gazelle

for all those years I couldn't dance
for all the pain that is both
near and far
already past
and still to come

I say to you
these are the moments I live for
the alive times
give me life
and I will drink it
like water.

I wouldn't trade the chaos within me
for all the boats in the world

I will drown in this water
blissfully
for it is life.

Finally

there is not enough music
in this night
the notes fly
faster, faster than anyone
can keep up with
but it is not
clutter

imperfect symmetry
there is logic here
I grasp it
because I sorely need
logic now.

too long have I been
awake
seeing everything
hearing beyond.

the orchestra
settles and tunes
the plaintive
reedy readiness
washes around me

suspended over
a pregnant pause
the overture trips out

and my brain
finally
quiets.

There Is So Much Light

the current flows
through me
and my bones
glint like steel
and my mind
sharp as blades
the electricity
is under my skin

the night
is dark
but there is so much
light in me

how could my life
ever be black again
when there is such
a strong beacon?

this signal fire
of my own
brain chemistry.

people were
my training wheels
but I am starting to pedal
on my own

no matter what
pits I may encounter
in the future
I know

I can make it through.
because
finally
finally
I see my own strength.

Chasing The Sky

hollowed out
sleepless eyes
shift restlessly
one foot tapping
leg bouncing

I've been split in two
the first me paces the ground
doggedly

the second has ascended
hovering in the sky
aglow, enlightened
have I earned my wings at last?

this angel reaches to me
"come, come with me
I know a place that will make you
celestial.

"like me,
a being of the sky
you will never be sad again."

my other half has become a god
and the pieces that are left behind
ache for the eminence
sovereignty

that surely I must be due

but as I watch him disappear
ever higher above me
I feel our connection
snap tight like a rubber band
and break
the letting go of him
feels like I have lost
my deepest soul.

I am me again
just me
not a god

at least,
not until the next time he returns.
and you wonder
why I chase the sky?

In Between

Tiny blonde girl
Tiny white dress
Out in the yard
She feels wind's caress

Singing her song
Childish and free
No one to care
No destiny

Where is that girl?
Was she really me?
There was so much
That she wanted to be

But I'm trying now
I'll get there somehow
Someday soon I'll move on
Stuck no longer
In between

Each day she grows
A song in her heart
She prays that her dream
Will not fall apart

She hides from the fear
Wants to live out loud

She tries to fit in
Make somebody proud

Who is that girl?
Was she really me?
There was so much
That she wanted to be

But I'm trying now
I'll get there somehow
Someday soon I'll move on
Stuck no longer
In between.

Seaworthy

I am
midnight's best customer
the anticipatory
blanket of silence
the isolating
sting of loneliness
the oppressive
stifling of being
locked indoors.

I was not made for this world
I am too large
too passionate
erratic
ecstatic

how can I fit into the shell
I am expected to,
relate to
others around me?

I have been places
you wouldn't believe
but only in my mind

my mind
a vessel that
isn't quite

seaworthy

I patch the cracks
again
and again
but still the seawater
leaks in
erodes away pieces
until what is left is
a rusted latticework
of missed connections.

but there is something beautiful
about this mess.
something haunting
hunting
like a song that just won't leave you

I don't mean to unseat you
or cause you unease
I just want someone to know me.

stay with me
and I will show you
this world.

It's Like I Think I Have Wings

boxed in feeling
like a cat in a cage
every night
as I lie awake
sit awake
pace awake

I can't help
thinking
that's what
gets me in trouble
the thinking
ideas
aspirations

I am king of the world
so sad Jack
I don't need a ship
a ladder
a damned
stepstool

it's like I think
I have wings
and one day I'm
going to try to fly
and I'd better hope
there's a damn big net

to catch me
when I do

Come With Me

come with me
she said
but I stood still

too many regrets
too much fear
the lines of reality
are sometimes
blurred.

come with me
she said
and I hesitated

not like she was
a stranger
I knew her
more intimately
than I knew myself.

come with me
she said
and slowly
I joined her.

you're flying,
she said
but where did I get

these wings?

Cunning

excuse me while I
clear the clouds
from my head.

How do you say no
to nothingness?

If you could make everything
slow down
for just a little while,
why wouldn't you?

The bustle of the world
the headlines
the deadlines
the screaming battle between
the thoughts in your head.

Even when things are quiet
you can hear it calling you

Red rover
Red rover
will Rex please come over?

And every time I say
no I won't
I can't

Every time I remember
that existing as a shell
that forgetting entire days
that accomplishing nothing
is barely existing at all

But I know It as I know myself
and the birds have eaten
my breadcrumb trail anyway
so It's all I've got.

It coaxed me out into these woods
with false promises
and our confrontation will happen here

as long as it's not too late.

Baffling

it warms my chest
a trickling supernova
like I'd just taken a shot
of vodka maybe

but the shadows
veil my mind
and my thoughts come out
disjointed.

every morning
I wake with a song
thrust forward with a drive
to live
to be alive.

every morning
I count all my bones
to make sure they are
all in their places

every morning
there are a thousand yesses
and a thousand nos
all tangled up like
the cat was playing with the yarn again

yes and no firmly

standing like a forest
and I've been
walking in circles for quite some time now.
I don't think the answer is here.

But the burning shot in my chest
is a soothing, sickly warmth
because when things are so precarious
I am frozen, and
there is no decision to be made

and I can only sink below the horizon
and disappear
for a little while.

Powerful

I climbed the thick tree trunk
scraping my skin raw on the bark
but I made it high into the air
but still it followed me.

I walked through fire with my bare feet
scorching my heels and charring my flesh
I made it across
but still it followed me.

Who is the more powerful,
it asks in a mocking voice.
For I will follow you
to the ends of the earth

I said to it,
that makes you tenacious
if you don't give up quickly
you can follow me wherever I go
but it won't mean a thing unless
I let you in.

I am not powerful
but I am not powerless.

You can follow me anywhere.
And I will do great things
because you are there

to remind me
where bottom is

and baby,
I'm the top.

Didn't You Know

didn't you know
that one word
one action
one thought
can change everything?

didn't you know
that when the night
feels endless
and you are so heavy
that you can't
get off the couch
you are not alone?

that flashing gleam
giddy midnights
that lead to
hopeless dawns
I know them too
it will all pass.

who was it that said
that suicide is painless?

perhaps they meant
that after all the
soul crushing
pain,

nothing could hurt
anymore

but even when
every breath is
a struggle
please

talk to someone

keep breathing

it will pass
it always does
no one is alone
there is always love
even when you think
you lost it

keep breathing
because something
beautiful
is coming.

ACKNOWLEDGEMENTS

There are so many people in my life that keep me going, keep me writing, keep me creating. The QSCC at McMaster University accepted me when I was questioning my gender and gave me my first taste of what it was like to really be me. The Theatre & Film program at McMaster also took me in like a child, and protected me in times where my mind strayed from the realms of normal. The cast of Midsummer Night's Dream 2013 surrounded me with love, which helped me move on, which helped me give birth to this book.

To everyone who has ever visited me in the hospital, those who made me laugh and forget the torment of the mind, and to those who sat quietly and let me know I wasn't alone.

To everyone who reached out, over phone, over facebook, in person, to make sure I was ok – I am ok. And I love you for that.

Life isn't meant to be lived alone. I've just been lucky enough to surround myself with the most amazing people.

Thank you.

Rex Emerson Jackson
2014